THE LOVE CHAPTER

D1551739

PUBLISHING

Torrance, California

The Love Chapter
© 2014 Bristol Works, Inc.

Rose Publishing, Inc.
4733 Torrance Blvd., #259
Torrance, California 90503 USA
www.rose-publishing.com

Printed in China by Regent Publishing Services Ltd.
May 2014, 1st printing

CONTENTS

LOVE REQUIRES COURAGE

1 Corinthians 13

First Corinthians 13 is one of the most beautiful, inspiring, and relevant passages in the New Testament. Its relevance lies in the very importance of relationships in our lives. God created us to be relational beings. Relationships are not optional. They are central to what it means to be human. We inevitably relate to God, nature, and each other. Love is what makes relationships possible. Love binds people in relationships.

However, we are broken people. Sin has affected our relationships. They are not what they should be: there is distrust, pain, anger, misunderstanding, fear, isolation, and abuse. We are afraid of being hurt—

so much so, that we hardly let anyone, including God, see us with our guard down. Fear has kept us from true intimacy and from deep, satisfying relationships.

How, then, can we feel safe to open our hearts and let others see who we are? The apostle Paul shows us "the most excellent way" to feel safe to open our hearts to others, and to be safe for others to open their hearts to us. The love that Paul describes fosters intimacy, openness, security, comfort, growth, and support. It is a love that is applicable to all areas of our lives: from spouses and children, to people inside and outside the church, to people we meet unexpectedly, accidentally, or temporarily in our daily activities. We are safe because God has shown this love to us through Christ, and the Spirit pours it in our hearts daily. He fills us with all the love we need. It is a love that "drives out fear" (1 John 4:18).

"God is love. Whoever lives in love lives in God, and God in them. This is how love is made complete among us so that we will have confidence on the day of judgment: In this world we are like Jesus. There is no fear in love. But perfect love drives out fear, because fear has to do with punishment. The one who fears is not made perfect in love. We love because he first loved us."—1 John 4:16b–19

1 Corinthians 13

If I speak in the tongues of men or of angels, but do not have love, I am only a resounding gong or a clanging cymbal. If I have the gift of prophecy and can fathom all mysteries and all knowledge, and if I have a faith that can move mountains, but do not have love, I am nothing. If I give all I possess to the poor and give over my body to hardship that I may boast, but do not have love, I gain nothing.

Love is patient, love is kind. It does not envy, it does not boast, it is not proud. It does not dishonor others, it is not self-seeking, it is not easily angered, it keeps no record of wrongs. Love does not delight in evil but rejoices with the truth. It always protects, always trusts, always hopes, always perseveres.

Love never fails. But where there are prophecies, they will cease; where there are tongues, they will be stilled; where there is knowledge, it will pass away. For we know in part and we prophesy in part, but when completeness comes, what is in part disappears. When I was a child, I talked like a child, I thought like a child, I reasoned like a child. When I became a man, I put the ways of childhood behind me. For now we see only a reflection as in a mirror; then we shall see face to face. Now I know in part; then I shall know fully, even as I am fully known.

And now these three remain: faith, hope and love. But the greatest of these is

Overview of 1 Corinthians 13

The beautiful words about love occur in the context of Paul's teachings about spiritual gifts. God gives spiritual gifts to his people for the benefit of the whole church. The apostle shows "the most excellent way" (1 Corinthians 12:31). That is, when God's people exercise their spiritual gifts in the context of love, they work the way God intends them.

1. *Gifts without Love* = *Nothing*

- Tongues
- Prophecy
- Knowledge
- Faith
- Martyrdom

2. *Definition of Love*

Love is
- Patient
- Kind

Love does not
- Envy
- Boast
- Keep record of wrongs
- Delight in evil

Love is not
- Proud
- Rude
- Self-seeking
- Easily angered

Love does
- Rejoice with the truth
- Protect always
- Trust always
- Hope always
- Persevere always

3. Love Never Fails

- Prophecy
- Tongues
- Knowledge

These gifts will end

Love is the perfect goal and fulfillment of

- Incomplete knowledge
- Incomplete prophesy
- Growth
- Sight/Recognition

Conclusion

Love is the greatest of eternal affections/ attitudes

FAITH   HOPE   LOVE

WHAT LOVE IS

v. 4 "Love is patient ... "

Love Is
Patient, steadfast, enduring

Definition
Willing to endure emotional discomfort and suffering. It is the opposite of demanding what we want right now and being easily angered.

Scripture
"Be patient, then, brothers and sisters, until the Lord's coming. See how the farmer waits for the land to yield its valuable crop, patiently waiting for the autumn and spring rains. You too, be patient and stand firm, because the Lord's coming is near. Don't grumble against one another, brothers and sisters, or you will be judged. The Judge is standing at the door!"—James 5:7–9

"The end of a matter is better than its beginning, and patience is better than pride."— Ecclesiastes 7:8

"But the fruit of the Spirit is love, joy, peace, forbearance, kindness, goodness, faithfulness, gentleness and self-control. Against such things there is no law."—Galatians 5:22–23

v. 4 " ... love is kind ... "

Love Is
Kind, good, pleasant

Definition
Seeking the best for the other person. Love is willing to go the extra mile. It is the opposite of being rude.

Scripture
"Be kind and compassionate to one another, forgiving each other, just as in Christ God forgave you."
—Ephesians 4:32

"Therefore, as God's chosen people, holy and dearly loved, clothe yourselves with compassion, kindness, humility, gentleness and patience."
—Colossians 3:12

"What does love look like? It has the hands to help others. It has the feet to hasten to the poor and needy. It has eyes to see misery and want. It has the ears to hear the sighs and sorrows of men. That is what love looks like."

—AUGUSTINE

v. 6 "Love ... rejoices with the truth"

Love Is
Rejoicing with truth

Definition
Happy to know what is true. It is the opposite of delighting in evil. Knowing and admitting the truth creates a reliable environment for the other person.

Scripture
"It has given me great joy to find some of your children walking in the truth, just as the Father commanded us."
—2 John 4

See also 3 John 3–4

v. 7 "It always protects ... "

Love Is
Always protective, preserving

Definition
Love reassures others that their heart is safe with us. It is the opposite of keeping a record of wrongs.

Scripture
"Brothers and sisters, if someone is caught in a sin, you who live by the Spirit should restore that person gently. But watch yourselves, or you also may be tempted. Carry each other's burdens, and in this way you will fulfill the law of Christ."—Galatians 6:1–2

See also 1 Corinthians 9:12

v. 7 "[Love] always trusts ... "

Love Is
Always trusting, believing, faithful

Definition
Trust and faithfulness are necessary for an open, intimate relationship. When people open up their hearts, they need to be safe and cared for, even when they disappoint you. It is the opposite of self-seeking.

Scripture
"May the God of hope fill you with all joy and peace as you trust in him, so that you may overflow with hope by the power of the Holy Spirit."
—Romans 15:13

"If we want the advantages of love, then we must be willing to take the risks of love. And that requires vulnerability. Of course, we can refuse this path and trod another one devoid of openness. But the toll on such a road is extremely high."

—CHARLES SWINDOLL

v. 7 "[Love] always hopes ... "

Love Is
Always hopeful, expectant, confident

Definition
Hopeful that, despite sin and mistakes, God blesses our faithfulness. Hopeful that, even if other people may abuse our trust, God will always be reliable. It is the opposite of a cynical, angry outlook.

Scripture
"Be strong and take heart, all you who hope in the Lord."—Psalm 31:24

See also Romans 15:13 and Joel 3:16

v. 7 "[Love] always perseveres ... "

Love Is
Always persevering, enduring, abiding

Definition
Despite wrongs and mistakes, love survives. Love makes people available to others, ready to listen, lend a hand, or be a comforting shoulder. It is the opposite of failing or falling.

Scripture
"Be joyful in hope, patient in affliction, faithful in prayer."—Romans 12:12

See also 1 Peter 2:20

WHAT LOVE IS *NOT*

v. 4 "It does not envy ... "

Love Is Not
Envious, jealous, covetous

Definition
Wanting to be what others are or to have what others have. It is possessiveness to the point of obsession, the opposite of *contentedness*.

Scripture
"Resentment kills a fool, and envy slays the simple."—Job 5:2

See also Psalm 37:1, Proverbs 27:4, 1 Timothy 6:4, and Titus 3:3

v. 4 "It does not boast ... "

Love Is Not
Boastful, bragging, conceited

Definition
Constantly talking about oneself in a conceited way. It is the opposite of quiet *humility*.

Scripture
"Likewise, the tongue is a small part of the body, but it makes great boasts. Consider what a great forest is set on fire by a small spark."—James 3:5

"As it is, you boast in your arrogant schemes. All such boasting is evil."—James 4:16

See also Psalm 10:3 and Proverbs 25:14

v. 4 " ... it is not proud ... "

Love Is Not
Proud, arrogant, egotistical

Definition
Having an inflated sense of the self, having a "big head." Living as if only *your* opinion, tastes, and choices matter. It is the opposite of *being humble*.

Scripture
"In the same way, you who are younger, submit yourselves to your elders. All of you, clothe yourselves with humility toward one another, because, 'God opposes the proud but shows favor to the humble.'"—1 Peter 5:5

See also Proverbs 16:5, Jeremiah 50:31–32, and James 4:6

v. 5 "It does not dishonor others ... "

Love Is Not
Rude, immodest, disgraceful

Definition
A lack of consideration for other's feelings or needs; insolent, offensive and provocative behavior. The attitude of being more important than others. It is the opposite of *kindness*.

Scripture
"The lips of the righteous know what finds favor, but the mouth of the wicked only what is perverse."—Proverbs 10:32

See also Romans 1:27, 1 Corinthians 7:36, and Revelation 16:15

"If I belittle those whom I am called to serve, talk of their weak points in contrast perhaps with what I think of as my strong points; if I adopt a superior attitude, forgetting 'Who made thee to differ? and what hast thou that thou hast not received?' then I know nothing of Calvary love."

—AMY CARMICHAEL

v. 5 " ... it is not self-seeking ... "

Love Is Not
Self-seeking, self-centered, selfish

Definition
"Looking out for number one," or being wrapped up in one's own concerns. It is the opposite of *a life centered on God*.

Scripture
"Do nothing out of selfish ambition or vain conceit. Rather, in humility value others above yourselves, not looking to your own interests but each of you to the interests of the others."
—Philippians 2:3–4

See also 1 Corinthians 10:24, 33 and Romans 15:1–2

v. 5 " ... it is not easily angered ... "

Love Is Not
Easily angered, irritable, provoked

Definition
Always ready for an argument, having a short fuse. It is the opposite of *patience and kindness*.

Scripture
"Do not be quickly provoked in your spirit, for anger resides in the lap of fools."—Ecclesiastes 7:9

See also Ephesians 4:31–32, Colossians 3:8, 21, and Titus 1:7

v. 5 " ... it keeps no record of wrongs."

Love Is Not
Keeping records of wrong, resentful

Definition
Unable to let go of past injustices, keeping a list of wrongs, and, often, planning revenge. Reminding others of how they have failed you in the past, and probably will in the future. It is the opposite of *being kind and forgiving*.

Scripture
"Do not say, 'I'll do to them as they have done to me; I'll pay them back for what they did.'"—Proverbs 24:29

See also Luke 9:53–55 and Colossians 3:13

"Assuredly there is but one way in which to achieve what is not merely difficult but utterly against human nature: to love those who hate us, to repay their evil deeds with benefits, to return blessings for reproaches. It is that we remember not to consider men's evil intention but to look upon the image of God in them, which cancels and effaces their transgressions, and with its beauty and dignity allures us to love and embrace them."

—JOHN CALVIN

v. 5 "Love does not delight in evil ... "

Love Is Not
Delighting in evil

Definition
Getting a kick out of other's troubles or the enjoyment of bad or twisted behavior. It is the opposite of *rejoicing in the truth*.

Scripture
"Although they know God's righteous decree that those who do such things deserve death, they not only continue to do these very things but also approve of those who practice them."
—Romans 1:32

POSITIVE QUALITIES

Patience

Patience is the ability to deal with a great deal of distress without becoming angry or annoyed. Patience is vital for deep, intimate, significant relationships. Understanding and accepting that we all are flawed people with weaknesses, inabilities, and foolish behaviors is the foundation for patience.

Being patient does not seem to be a natural quality. It takes intention, practice, trial and error, and prayer. A patient person creates the space and acceptance that other people need to blossom and thrive as individuals.

Example
Job 1:13–21

Job was a very patient man. He dealt with a lot of emotional and physical discomfort.

What to Do
Think about something or someone that "pushes your buttons." Plan out how you are going to practice patience the next time you encounter that situation.

Kindness

"Giving until it hurts," is how Teresa of Calcutta defined love.

A kind heart goes the extra mile to show its love. When we show kindness, we give until it hurts; we keep the other person's feelings and needs at the front of our minds. Kindness, then, becomes a way to show how much the other person means to us.

Often, a thoughtful, kind word can cause anger to dissolve and allow a relationship to repair. Kind words and actions can soothe a hurting or resentful heart. They can open the door to reconciliation and healing.

Example
Joshua 2:6–16

Rahab showed kindness to the Israelite spies by hiding them from danger. As a result, her family was saved from the destruction of Jericho.

What to Do
Ask God to help you to think of several persons who might benefit from an act of kindness. Plan how you will make this happen.

Giving and Love

Giving brings us freedom.

If you want to be free from materialism and the love of money, start by giving. When we release our grip on money and possessions, we break free from the grip they have on our lives. Giving keeps us from spiraling down the destructive path of greed.

"For the love of money is a root of all kinds of evil. Some people, eager for money, have wandered from the faith and pierced themselves with many griefs."
—1 Timothy 6:10

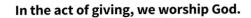

In the act of giving, we worship God.

When we give we acknowledge that it is ultimately God's money and it is his right to instruct us how to use it. Theologian Richard Foster suggests that rather than approaching the question of giving as "How much of my money should I give God?" we should ask, "How much of God's money should I keep for myself?"

"Suppose a brother or a sister is without clothes and daily food. If one of you says to them, 'Go in peace; keep warm and well fed,' but does nothing about their physical needs, what good is it? In the same way, faith by itself, if it is not accompanied by action, is dead."—James 2:15–17

Giving makes us put our trust where in belongs—in our God.

Stockpiling possessions may be a sign of trusting in the things we have rather than trusting in God. Giving helps focus one's eyes back on God, seeking him as the first priority and relying on him to supply our needs.

Following Jesus requires earthly sacrifice for heavenly gain. Christian author Randy Alcorn says, "The more holdings we have on earth, the more likely we are to forget that we're citizens of another world ... and our inheritance lies there, not here."

"Sell your possessions and give to the poor. Provide purses for yourselves that will not wear out, a treasure in heaven that will never fail, where no thief comes near and no moth destroys."—Luke 12:33

Giving is a privilege which comes from love.

Whether we have been blessed with much or with little, we can be part of God's plan. Financial giving is one of many ways to do the Lord's work. As God has blessed you, you can bless others. God gave generously to us out of his great love, and we give generously out of our love for others.

"Whoever is kind to the poor lends to the Lord, and he will reward them for what they have done."—Proverbs 19:17

"The generous will themselves be blessed, for they share their food with the poor."—Proverbs 22:9

"You can give without loving, but you cannot love without giving."

—AMY CARMICHAEL

Rejoicing with the Truth

We are broken people, and we deal with broken people. We can rejoice knowing that despite the evil within us, God loved us and we can love each other. Truth frees us to deal with each other in realistic, compassionate, kind ways. It allows us to see ourselves the way God sees us. Then we can help each other improve and carry each other's burdens.

Truth should never be a weapon to hurt others; rather, it is an opportunity to know each other better. Ultimately, rejoicing in the truth is rejoicing in Christ, who is Truth.

Example
Exodus 18:1–27

Moses' father-in-law, Jethro, visited the Israelites' camp in the wilderness. Jethro noticed that Moses was overworked and overwhelmed. He corrected Moses and advised him to train other people who could help him. Instead of hearing criticism, rejection, and judgment, Moses accepted his father-in-law's advice. Jethro spoke truth to Moses out of love and concern; by accepting Jethro's advice, Moses showed his joy in truth.

What to Do

Take an inventory of your own life. List the positive qualities that God can use for his purposes (see the lists of gifts in Romans 12, 1 Corinthians 12, and Ephesians 4 and fruits of the Spirit in Galatians 5:16–25). Then make a list of areas of your life that need changing. Make an honest assessment of your character, your conversations, your use of money and other things, and your relationships. How can the truth of your life help you be a better person with better relationships?

Protective

We are all afraid of betrayal and hurt; we need to feel safe and needed if we are to open our hearts to others. When people open their hearts to us, we must protect them with the greatest care. We show our willingness to protect them by bearing their errors in a forgiving way and by refusing to expose their weaknesses or mistakes.

Example
2 Samuel 9

David was protective of the family of his best friend Jonathan, even after some difficult times.

What to Do
Identify some ways in which you would have benefited by more protection. Plan a way to pass on that protection to someone else.

Trustful

Only when we trust people are we able to open our hearts and become vulnerable. Breaking someone's trust ruins relationships. Only when we are truthful can we be trusted. When we deal truthfully with each other, our hearts rejoice knowing that our inner beings are safe, that our most treasured secrets, desires, and needs will not be abused.

Example
Esther 2

Esther was a young woman when she was plunged into royal life in Persia. During this time, Esther relied on her cousin Mordecai's advice and support. Without him, her life in the court would have been very different.

What to Do

Trust grows over time. If we can be trustworthy with the small things, people will entrust us with the deep things of the heart as well. Pay attention to the ways people are offering their trust. Gossip, sarcasm, or small criticisms can wreck other people's trust in us.

"Love anything and your heart will be wrung and possibly broken. If you want to make sure of keeping it intact you must give it to no one, not even an animal. Wrap it carefully round with hobbies and little luxuries; avoid all entanglements. Lock it up safe in the casket or coffin of your selfishness. But in that casket—safe, dark, motionless, airless— it will change. It will not be broken; it will become unbreakable, impenetrable, irredeemable. To love is to be vulnerable."

—C. S. Lewis

Hopeful

We will make mistakes, hurt others and get hurt. Often things look grim; it is easy to despair. However, because we can trust in God's faithfulness, we can hope that the Holy Spirit will intervene and guide us. Our hopefulness is not just optimism; rather, it is based on God's own faithfulness. It is that hope that will strengthen us to forgive, to trust again, to go on.

Example
Ruth 1

When Naomi's husband and children died, Naomi was left with only her two daughters-in-law, Orpah and Ruth. Naomi fell into distress and hopelessness. Ruth's faithfulness and courage brought hope to Naomi.

What to Do

What is your only hope in life and death? Identify ways you can be a more hopeful, confident person based on the hope you have in Christ.

Persevering

Always persevering: When we are patient, kind, truthful, protective, trusting, and hopeful, our love can weather storms that seem impossible. Since our hearts crave connections, they need assurance that the people we are connected to will be there. Perseverance does not mean that love will put up with injustice or evil. Love will do what is necessary to preserve a loving relationship.

Example

God's love is the best example of a love that perseveres. Despite our unfaithfulness, rebellion, and offenses, God continues to love us. His love is shown in Jesus giving his life for us.

What to Do

How do you make love last? Remember what led you to the relationship. Renew the commitment. Equipped with faith and hope, we can move on with the adventure of loving others and being loved.

"For God so loved the world that he gave his one and only Son, that whoever believes in him shall not perish but have eternal life."—John 3:16

"May the power of your love, Lord Christ, fiery and sweet as honey, so absorb our hearts as to withdraw them from all that is under heaven. Grant that we may be ready to die for love of your love, as you died for love of our love."

—FRANCIS OF ASSISI

NEGATIVE QUALITIES

Love is a difficult feeling to express in words. Exploring what love is *not* can help us to get a picture of what love actually *is*.

Love Is Not Envious

Envy destroys relationships. Envy brings mistrust and betrayal. The focus of an envious heart is itself. When we are overcome with envy, we are focusing on our interests and desires (James 3:14, 16).

What It Leads To
Envy leads one to bitterness, selfishness, anger, and other evils.

Example
Genesis 4:3–8

Cain's envy of his brother led to murder.

"Do not be like Cain, who belonged to the evil one and murdered his brother. And why did he murder him? Because his own actions were evil and his brother's were righteous."—1 John 3:12

What to Do

When you find yourself envious of others, try praying for them. Thank God for his care for them and ask him to continue to bless them.

A Word about Envy

Although we often use the words *envy, jealousy,* and *covetousness* as synonymous, they are quite different.

Envy
(a) The desire and resentment of what other people have or are.

(b) It harbors anger, ill intentions, and the hope of undoing what others have or are.

Jealousy
(a) The fear of losing what we consider rightfully ours.

(b) It results in anger or withdrawal as means to protect the loss of what we consider precious. It may be a normal feeling; a warning signal—as in the dashboard of our cars—that tells of the danger of losing a loved one.

Covetousness

(a) Dissatisfaction of what we have that leads to wanting to have other things.

(b) It is an offense against God—thus the reason it is in the Ten Commandments—because it presumes that we know better than God what we need and is good for us. It becomes a rebellious and idolatrous action by putting ourselves in the place of God (Eph. 5:5).

"But godliness with contentment is great gain. For we brought nothing into the world, and we can take nothing out of it."
—1 Timothy 6:6–7

"I am not saying this because I am in need, for I have learned to be content whatever the circumstances. I know what it is to be in need, and I know what it is to have plenty. I have learned the secret of being content in any and every situation, whether well fed or hungry, whether living in plenty or in want. I can do all this through him who gives me strength."—Philippians 4:11–13

"If we only wanted to be happy it would be easy; but we want to be happier than other people, which is almost always difficult, since we think them happier than they are."

—CHARLES-LOUIS DE SECONDAT, BARON DE LA BRÈDE ET DE MONTESQUIEU

Love Is Not Boastful

Love is not self-absorbed. Constant boasting ignores the fact that all blessings and good gifts come from God. It also ignores how much we depend on and owe others. Boasting destroys love by ignoring others' contributions to our lives. It pretends to be independent and pushes people away.

What It Leads To

Boasting can lead to an unrealistic or false opinion of oneself. Such an opinion may lead one to belittle, dismiss, or insult others. It may further lead one to a proud heart.

Example

1 Samuel 17

Goliath lost his head over a boast.

What to Do

Try breaking the habit of boasting by talking about others' good deeds or qualities. Better yet, "boast about Jesus."

"For we do not want to boast about work already done in someone else's territory. But, 'Let the one who boasts boast in the Lord.' For it is not the one who commends himself who is approved, but the one whom the Lord commends."
— 2 Corinthians 10:16b–18

Love Is Not Proud

We often hear, "be proud of yourself." A clear understanding of one's strengths is good; however, pride can get out of control. Arrogance and egotism show an inflated, "puffed up" sense of the self. Love needs a realistic, honest, and open attitude about oneself.

What It Leads To

Although pride may begin as a desire to be better, it can lead to an excessive love of our own excellence. Pride destroys relationships and leads to lack of modesty and humility, foolishness, and abusive, rude behavior toward others.

Example

Daniel 4:28–37

King Nebuchadnezzar was humbled because of his pride.

What to Do

Ask God to give you an accurate picture of yourself. Thank him for the good things about you and ask him for help in the problem areas. Do not be fearful of having to change. Ask God for help to make those changes work.

PROVERBS ABOUT PRIDE
AND HUMILITY

"Pride goes before destruction, a haughty spirit before a fall."
—Proverbs 16:18

"He mocks proud mockers but shows favor to the humble and oppressed."—Proverbs 3:34

"Wisdom's instruction is to fear the Lord, and humility comes before honor."—Proverbs 15:33

"Do not boast about tomorrow, for you do not know what a day may bring."—Proverbs 27:1

"Pride brings a person low, but the lowly in spirit gain honor."
—Proverbs 29:23

"Better to be lowly in spirit along with the oppressed than to share plunder with the proud."
—PROVERBS 16:19

"Humility is the fear of the LORD; its wages are riches and honor and life."—PROVERBS 22:4

"Where there is strife, there is pride, but wisdom is found in those who take advice."
—PROVERBS 13:10

"A fool's mouth lashes out with pride, but the lips of the wise protect them."—PROVERBS 14:13

"When pride comes, then comes disgrace, but with humility comes wisdom."—PROVERBS 11:2

Love Is Not Rude

A lack of consideration for others' feelings or needs is the beginning of disrespectful, offensive, and provocative behavior. In our society, rude behavior has become a way to succeed or be popular for some. Rudeness hurts relationships. When we ignore feelings or needs, people feel rejected, unwanted, abandoned.

What It Leads To

Rude behavior may begin as a reaction to a felt or real offense, a way to protect our vulnerability, to keep others away when we feel threatened. It may also try to hide over-confidence, a false sense of independence, and limitations. Rude behavior, however, causes anger, hurt, fear, and disconnection from others.

Example
Genesis 3:10

Shame is a natural response to bad behavior. Adam and Eve first felt it when they disobeyed God.

Zephaniah 3:1–5

God warns against rude, shameless behavior.

What to Do
If you wonder whether you have lost your sense of shame, try putting yourself in other people's shoes. How do you feel when someone is rude to you? Ask God to restore your conscience.

Love Is Not Self-seeking

The concern for oneself above others' needs may begin as an attempt to shore up a false self-image. Selfishness destroys relationships because we become incapable of seeing others' needs and desires. Our consuming desire to fulfill our every need leads us away from others.

What It Leads To

Selfishness leads to resentment, anger, and broken relationships. Unless we are willing to see life from others' perspectives, we will be limited in the depth and beauty of our relationships.

Example

"People will be lovers of themselves, lovers of money, boastful, proud, abusive, disobedient to their parents, ungrateful, unholy ..."—2 Timothy 3:2

God warns us that people who reject him will become lovers of themselves.

Paul tells us to seek after the good of others rather than ourselves.

"No one should seek their own good, but the good of others."
—1 Corinthians 10:24

What to Do

Ask God to help you think of the needs of others. Plan a strategy for doing something for someone every day for the next week.

"Since love grows within you, so beauty grows. For love is the beauty of the soul."

—AUGUSTINE

"Often the only thing a child can remember about an adult in later years, when he or she is grown, is whether or not that person was kind."

—BILLY GRAHAM

Love Is Not
Easily Angered

When we feel insecure, threatened, ignored, or offended, anger is a natural reaction. The emotion of anger itself is not evil—even God gets angry with injustice and arrogance. The problem is an anger that takes over our minds and hearts, lashing out to hurt the other person. This anger destroys relationships and hurts people deeply.

What It Leads To

Feeling anger over serious wrongs is understandable. However, quick angry responses lead to more anger and, often, to verbal or physical violence. Uncontrollable anger causes fear, resentment, and withdrawal from the relationship.

Example
1 Kings 21

King Ahab's anger led to murder and eventually the downfall of his kingdom.

What to Do
Try thinking about the real cause(s) of your anger. Ask God to help you deal with those issues in a constructive way. Try finding ways to deal with the emotion when it flares up.

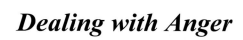

Dealing with Anger

Anger is a natural response when we are harmed. But God's Word says to be careful that our anger does not result in taking revenge. We should not add sin upon sin, but leave the situation where it belongs—in God's hands.

"Do not say, 'I'll pay you back for this wrong!' Wait for the Lord, and he will avenge you."
—Proverbs 20:22

"In your anger do not sin: Do not let the sun go down while you are still angry, and do not give the devil a foothold."
—Ephesians 4:26–27

Sometimes anger and bitterness prevent us from experiencing the freedom of forgiveness. The following steps can help us break free from the chains of anger.

1. Acknowledge God's complete forgiveness by grace.

"For he has rescued us from the dominion of darkness and brought us into the kingdom of the Son he loves, in whom we have redemption, the forgiveness of sins."— Colossians 1:13–14

I am forgiven by the grace of God!

2. Be willing to confess your bitterness and resentment to God.

"Create in me a pure heart, O God, and renew a steadfast spirit within me. Do not cast me from your presence or take your Holy Spirit from me. Restore to me the joy of your salvation and grant me a willing spirit, to sustain me." —Psalm 51:10–12

God, forgive my bitter attitudes and my anger toward _____.

3. Recognize that your anger is a violation of God's Word and choose to release the anger.

"For if you forgive other people when they sin against you, your heavenly Father will also forgive you. But if you do not forgive others their sins, your Father will not forgive your sins."
— Matthew 6:14–15

"Make every effort to live in peace with everyone and to be holy; without holiness no one will see the Lord. See to it that no one falls short of the grace of God and that no bitter root grows up to cause trouble and defile many."
— Hebrews 12:14–15

With the Holy Spirit's help, I choose to lay down this anger. I release my desire for revenge on _____.

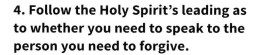

4. Follow the Holy Spirit's leading as to whether you need to speak to the person you need to forgive.

"Speak and act as those who are going to be judged by the law that gives freedom, because judgment without mercy will be shown to anyone who has not been merciful. Mercy triumphs over judgment." —James 2:12–13

God, I ask for your Spirit to guide me into what I should do next.

Go through these steps repeatedly until words become experience.

Love Does Not Keep a Record of Wrongs

Pretending everything is okay only causes resentment. It may seem easier to avoid conflict, to retreat and hide, to pretend things are well. However, until we have dealt with the deep things of the heart, we will not have forgiven. When we cannot forgive, we keep a detailed track of all the offenses the other person has done against us. Relationships cannot survive such resentment.

What It Leads To

Keeping a record of wrongs leads to deep resentment and inner bitterness. A disgruntled heart can turn into a heart that plans evil against the other. When people reach this point, relationships are truly in danger of perishing. Forgiveness is critical.

Example
1 Samuel 18, 19, 24, and 26

Saul held a grudge against David that led to plans and attempts against David's life. Yet, it was Saul who lost his life and kingdom in the end.

Jesus took God's true record of our wrongs and "nailed it to the cross." That is, he paid the price for us.

"You were dead because of your sins and because your sinful nature was not yet cut away. Then God made you alive with Christ, for he forgave all our sins. He canceled the record of the charges against us and took it away by nailing it to the cross."—Colossians 2:13–14 NLT

What to Do

Think about what Jesus did for you. He took God's true record about your sin and paid it for you by his death. Forgiving others may not be easy, but it is the least you can do in gratitude. Try imagining that all the things that have hurt you are in the bottom of the ocean—gone forever.

"*Resentment is like a glass of poison that a man drinks; then he sits down and waits for his enemy to die.*"

—ANONYMOUS

"*Forgiveness is unlocking a door to set someone free and realizing you were the prisoner!*"

—ANONYMOUS

How to Forgive

1. Examine your own sin.

Recognizing our own need for God's forgiveness enables us to see our offender's need for mercy. Self-righteousness will breed an unforgiving heart, but through humility we can learn to extend mercy to others.

"Whoever conceals their sins does not prosper, but the one who confesses and renounces them finds mercy."
—Proverbs 28:13

2. Learn from veteran forgivers.

There is no cookie-cutter way to forgive. Every situation is different. For instance, how to go about forgiving a close friend who has betrayed you will be different from how to forgive an unknown hit-and-run driver. We can gain wisdom in knowing how to deal with particular situations by taking note of Christians who have already walked the path of forgiveness. Their examples and guidance can give us a long-term view beyond the initial feelings of anger and pain.

"Join together in following my example, brothers and sisters, and just as you have us as a model, keep your eyes on those who live as we do."—Philippians 3:17

3. Let forgiveness take time.

The apostle Paul compares the Christian life to a race that we have not yet finished. This side of heaven we may not be able to forgive to the extent that we want to because we are still imperfect people in an imperfect world. What we are called to do is to continue moving forward and not to give up.

"Not that I have already obtained all this, or have already arrived at my goal, but I press on to take hold of that for which Christ Jesus took hold of me." —Philippians 3:12

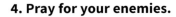

4. Pray for your enemies.

It might sound cliché to say "just pray about it," but there is nothing trite about praying for someone who has wronged you. Such prayers can have a powerful effect on the person praying. By the power of God's Spirit in us, through prayer, God can miraculously change our hatred into love.

Loving your "enemies" is to see them as fellow human beings who are loved by God and in need of his grace; but it is not to tolerate their abuse or invite them to hurt you again. The so-called "love" that ignores or allows such damaging sins is not really love at all.

"But I tell you, love your enemies and pray for those who persecute you, that you may be children of your Father in heaven."
—Matthew 5:44–45a

*"That is the whole lesson:
the sins of others you see,
but your own sin you fail to
see. In repentance, recognize
God's mercy toward you;
in this way alone will you be
able to forgive."*

—DIETRICH BONHOEFFER

Love Does Not Delight in Evil

Many people do not rejoice in doing evil. However, delighting in evil can be as simple as rejoicing when things do not go well for others. When our hearts are filled with resentment, anger, hatred, and discontent, it is easier to wish evil for others; it is easy to find joy in witnessing suffering and grief in other people.

What It Leads To

When we allow our hearts to find joy in evil, to rejoice in doing or allowing what is not right, we become increasingly deaf to the voice of the Holy Spirit.

Example

Daniel 6

The king's officers were so full of envy and hatred toward Daniel that they planned to kill him to get him out of the way. Only God's miraculous intervention prevented Daniel from dying in the den of lions.

What to Do

Having delighted in or planned evil against someone requires heartfelt repentance. Only the power of the Holy Spirit can lead us back to God's gentle embrace. To restore relationships with other people and God, we need forgiveness, faith, hope, and, above all, love.

THE FOUR LOVES

The New Testament uses two different words to express the concept of love. Ancient Greek had four different words that express fine distinctions of the concept love. Although the differences are not always clear, they were generally used in the following way:

Agape

- In Ancient Greek, *agape* was used more generally for a general affection for people or things.

- The New Testament uses the word *agape* in a special way. *Agape* is the selfless, unconditional, deep love that Christ embodied.

- *Agape* is the love that God showed for his creation (John 3:16), for Christ (John 17:26), and for those who believe in Jesus (John 14:21). *Agape* is also the love that believers should have for each other (1 John 4:17–18).

Phileo

- It is also known as "brotherly love."

- It is not as common in the New Testament as *agape*.

- *Phileo* refers to the affection for and response to people—family and friends—or activities one enjoys (1 Cor. 16:22; John 11:3, 5; 13:23; 16:27).

Eros

- This word does not appear in the New Testament.

- *Eros* refers to the love, passion, and attraction between lovers. It refers more generally to romantic love.

Storge

- This word does not appear in the New Testament.

- It was primarily used to describe the affection between family members— for example, the natural love of parents toward children.

"Christ did not teach and suffer that we might become, even in the natural loves, more careful of our own happiness. If a man is not uncalculating towards the earthly beloveds whom he has seen, he is none the more likely to be so towards God whom he has not. We shall draw nearer to God, not by trying to avoid the sufferings inherent in all loves, but by accepting them and offering them to Him; throwing away all defensive armour. If our hearts need to be broken, and if He chooses this as the way in which they should break, so be it."

—C. S. LEWIS (THE FOUR LOVES)

THE PRACTICE
OF LOVE

Love as Patience

Take time to listen to someone if they have a difficulty.

Overlook errors of others when they are trying hard and when the error is not damaging.

When someone comes to talk, give your full attention. Don't take phone calls while you are thus engaged.

Love as Kindness

Don't talk about people behind their backs or reveal a confidence even if it is true information.

Care about the wants, desires, and requests of the people around you. Look for creative ways of solving them.

Be polite and respectful even when others are frustrated and angry.

Love as Happy with the Truth
Give explanations, not excuses.

Play fair. Look for a win-win outcome.

Respectfully offer alternatives when asked to do something that is foolish or wrong.

Love as Protective
Be loyal. Don't encourage complaints. Listen to complaints, but do not add to them.

Be honest about past actions but do not destroy anyone's reputation.

Love as Trusting

Give people the benefit of the doubt. Treat people as though you believe in them.

Ask permission. Remember, trust is not presumption.

Love as Hopeful

Don't complain or whine. Be as confident and upbeat as the situation will allow.

Remember, even in a bad situation, our hope is ultimately in God.

Love as Persevering

Don't dominate or attract attention to yourself, but quietly strive for what is best.

Work hard and set the example.

Never give up. It is never wrong to do the loving thing!

"The rule for all of us is perfectly simple. Do not waste time bothering whether you love your neighbour; act as if you did. As soon as we do this we find one of the great secrets. When you are behaving as if you loved someone, you will presently come to love him. If you injure someone you dislike, you will find yourself disliking him more. If you do him a good turn, you will find yourself disliking him less."

—C. S. LEWIS (*MERE CHRISTIANITY*)

You Might Also Like

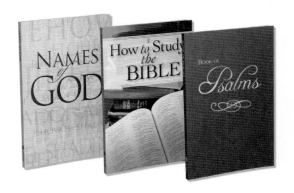

Names of God
ISBN: 9781628620863

How to Study the Bible
ISBN: 9781628620856

Book of Psalms
ISBN: 9781628620832